Grace, Period.
STUDY GUIDE

Grace, Period.
STUDY GUIDE

ROBERT MORRIS

NEW YORK   NASHVILLE

FaithWords
Hachette Book Group
1290 Avenue of the Americas, New York, NY 10104
faithwords.com
twitter.com/faithwords

First Edition: April 2024

FaithWords is a division of Hachette Book Group, Inc. The FaithWords name and logo are trademarks of Hachette Book Group, Inc.

The publisher is not responsible for websites (or their content) that are not owned by the publisher.

The Hachette Speakers Bureau provides a wide range of authors for speaking events. To find out more, go to hachettespeakersbureau.com or email HachetteSpeakers@hbgusa.com.

All Scripture quotations are taken from the New King James Version. Copyright®, © 1982 by Thomas Nelson. Used by permission. All rights reserved.

FaithWords books may be purchased in bulk for business, educational, or promotional use. For information, please contact your local bookseller or the Hachette Book Group Special Markets Department at special.markets@hbgusa.com.

ISBN: 9781546004943

Printed in the United States of America

LSC-C

Printing 1, 2024

CONTENTS

Part 3: Sons and Daughters, Period.

INTRODUCTION

We are delighted that you have chosen to use this study guide that was designed as a companion to the book *Grace, Period.* The lessons, principles, and stories are meant to help you look with fresh eyes at this amazing gift from God called grace and explore what it tells us about the Father-heart of God and His inconceivable love for us. One of the most impactful and transformative shifts you can make as a believer is to get your mind and heart around this simple but powerful truth: Grace is the unmerited, undeserved, unearned kindness and favor of God. No matter where you find yourself—whether you're a new believer, or you consider yourself a seasoned servant of the faith, or maybe you don't know what you are—I'm so thankful you have decided to take this journey to enjoying the abundant life God sent Jesus to purchase for us. A life given to us by grace—only grace.

How you use this study guide will depend on the purpose you have in mind. You can work through it on your own for personal development or as a part of a small study or discussion group. As you use this study to reflect on your life, we encourage you to read each chapter in *Grace, Period.* before you complete the exercises in the corresponding chapter in this study guide. Many of the questions are personal, and taking the time to read through the chapters in the book and think through how each question can affect your life will give the study immediate personal application. If you decide to use this study guide in a small group, go through each chapter on your own as preparation before each meeting. This will give your group study depth and make the sessions more productive for all.

Because of the personal nature of this study, if you use this guide in a group setting, remember that courtesy and mutual respect lay the foundation for a healthy group. A small group should be a safe place for all who participate. Some of what will be shared might be highly sensitive in nature, so respect the confidentiality of the person who is sharing. Don't let your conversations leave the small group. A small group is not a place to tell others what they should have done or said or thought, and it's not a place to force opinions on others. Commit yourselves to listening in love to one another, to praying for and supporting one another, to being sensitive to everyone's perspectives, and to showing each participant the grace you would like to receive from others.

It's Grace...Period.

1. What was your immediate response to the statement "the sheer wondrous, hilarious joy of generosity. Not 'giving to get,' but rather giving from a pure heart of gratitude for salvation in Jesus"? To what degree would you say that this level of generosity is true for you?

_____

_____

_____

_____

2. Describe a situation where you gave not to get but simply out of gratitude for what God has done for you. What impact did that have on you at the time?

_____

_____

_____

3. If you were the woman who received the financial gift, how do you think you would have reacted? Explain your thoughts.

_____

_____

_____

_____

_____

4. Why do most of us have such a hard time receiving a gift that is joyfully given from God, a gift given with nothing expected in return?

_____

_____

_____

_____

5. What is your definition of grace? More important, describe your practical experience with grace on a daily basis. Write an honest answer.

_____

_____

_____

_____

_____

6. When you think of the goodness and love of God, does its immensity stagger your mind? How do you feel knowing that He has adopted you into His family?

_____

_____

_____

_____

7. On a scale of 1 to 10, with 1 being that you strongly prefer to try to earn or merit God's love, and 10 being that you are delighted to simply receive it with open arms and a heart filled with gratitude, how would you grade yourself? Explain your answer.

_____

_____

_____

_____

8. Write out Luke 12:32 and begin to commit it to memory. How do you feel knowing this? Spend some time giving thanks to the Lord and share with Him how this blesses you.

_____

_____

_____

_____

9. What do you hope to discover as you read this book?

_____

_____

_____

_____

_____

PART 1

AMAZING, PERIOD.

CHAPTER 1

WHAT'S SO AMAZING?

1. Write out your personal experience of God's grace. Where do you feel you are in your relationship with God today?

_____

_____

_____

_____

2. Have you ever heard someone talking about the nature of God's grace or gotten into a discussion with someone who had a different viewpoint? How was their view different?

_____

_____

_____

_____

3. Did you find their viewpoint disturbing? Explain your thoughts.

_____

_____

_____

_____

_____

4. What makes the truth of grace so simple and yet so profound?

_____

_____

_____

_____

_____

5. What is so amazing about grace?

_____

_____

_____

_____

_____

_____

6. How does an understanding of grace change a person's life?

_____

_____

_____

_____

_____

7. Would you say that grace has elevated you to a closeness and intimacy with God as your Father? Take some time to reflect on this and write an honest answer.

_____

_____

_____

_____

_____

8. Do you feel weighted down in shame and condemnation and exhausted from trying to earn God's love? To what degree? Why do you think that is?

_____

_____

_____

_____

_____

9. Is the abundant, lavish, extravagant grace of God the best news in the world to you? How so?

_____

_____

_____

_____

10. What is the truth about our salvation? What does Colossians 2:6 tell us about it?

_____

_____

_____

_____

11. Do you feel like you need to add something to grace, or that there's a "but" that limits grace? Describe what you tend to add or subtract to grace.

_____

_____

_____

_____

12. Do you believe the key to an abundant life in Jesus is "Grace…
Period"? Or would you like to believe it? Write a prayer to the Lord telling
Him how you feel as you reflect on these truths.

_____

_____

_____

_____

_____

_____

CHAPTER 2

GIFT, WAGE, OR REWARD?

1. There are many theological views of the nature of grace. What are your thoughts on the view that believers are gifted, by God's "grace," with a set of oars with which we can row against the current pulling toward hell and get to heaven—providing, of course, we choose to use them, and row hard enough, consistently enough, till the very end?

_____

_____

_____

_____

2. If grace is defined as "unmerited favor," what is the problem with this divine enablement view?

_____

_____

_____

3. Has this been your view of grace, or do you know people who hold this view? How does it impact someone's life?

_____

_____

_____

_____

4. Bottom line: Our entrance into heaven is based upon what? Is there any indication that pulling our oars figures into the equation?

_____

_____

_____

_____

5. What were your thoughts about the other illustration that we are to use both an oar of grace and an oar of works and/or good behavior to cross the lake of life and arrive on heaven's shore? Does that accommodate the anticipated objection to Ephesians 2:8? Why not?

_____

_____

_____

_____

6. What are the terrifying implications of both these metaphors?

_____

_____

_____

_____

_____

7. Has fear of not being good enough to get to heaven or to receive the abundant life Jesus promised been used in your life to keep you toeing the line? Describe the bondage it brings. How is this the opposite of what Paul states in Romans 8:15–16?

_____

_____

_____

_____

_____

_____

8. More than 140 times in our English New Testaments, the Greek word *charis* is translated "grace." Define *charis* and describe its usage.

_____

_____

_____

_____

9. How does the related word *charisma* make the connection to the concept of "gift" plain? What are the only two things you can do with a gift?

_____

_____

_____

_____

_____

10. Write out and reflect upon Paul's bedrock definition of the means of our salvation in Ephesians 2:8–9. What role do we play in it?

_____

_____

_____

_____

_____

11. Grace is the unmerited, undeserved, unearned kindness and favor of God. What is its message of hope for you today and for the future?

_____

_____

_____

_____

CHAPTER 3

AMAZINGLY UNMERITED

1. What does the biblical term *boasting* or general term *bragging* mean?

_____

_____

_____

_____

2. Boasting may be an indicator of pride, but what does it indicate more often? If someone is constantly talking about their skills and accomplishments, what are they actually expressing?

_____

_____

_____

_____

3. "Grace is unmerited." Describe what the whole merit-badge system is built upon and what it means. Is that a bad thing? Do you find that you have a strong drive to achieve and merit rewards? Explain your thoughts.

_____

_____

_____

_____

_____

4. Break down Ephesians 2:8–9 by its phrases. What stands out to you? What boasting does it allow for when it comes to salvation? Why?

_____

_____

_____

_____

_____

5. There is a constant stream of boasting on earth about accomplishments and merits. How about in heaven today? How about in heaven forever? Any merit badges there?

_____

_____

_____

_____

_____

6. As an adopted son or daughter of God, what will keep any sense of merit from ever crossing your mind in heaven? What will be your testimony there forever?

_____

_____

_____

_____

7. When you've lived in sinfulness and depravity for years and then encounter the extravagant mercy of God—a mercy made available only through the enormous sacrifice of His sinless Son—you _know_ you don't merit it. What so easily happens, though, in the years that follow? Have you struggled with this? How so?

_____

_____

_____

_____

8. Describe the best thing you've ever done. Did you think that it surely must merit some favor, some blessing from God? What does Isaiah 64:6 say about what you've done?

_____

_____

_____

_____

9. Read Revelation 5:11–14. Describe the severe beauty of grace depicted there. Is there any hint of boasting among the "ten thousand times ten thousand, and thousands of thousands" gathered there?

_____

_____

_____

_____

_____

10. What valuable lesson about grace can you take from the yearbook story?

_____

_____

_____

_____

_____

11. "Love will cover a multitude of sins" (1 Peter 4:8). Describe a time when someone covered a sin or a stupid mistake you made. How did that make you feel?

_____

_____

_____

_____

_____

12. What is the difference between mercy and grace? How has God shown you His mercy? How has He shown you His grace?

_____

_____

_____

_____

_____

_____

13. Based on what you have learned in this chapter, take a moment and reflect on how you can start living every day knowing that God's grace is, indeed, unmerited.

_____

_____

_____

_____

_____

_____

CHAPTER 4

AMAZINGLY UNDESERVED

1. The Greek word translated "grace" in our English Bibles is *charis*. When most people in the first-century world read Ephesians 2:8 and saw, "For by [*charis*] you have been saved, through faith," how did they know that word carried a very specific bundle of meanings, references, and images long before it first appeared in the Bible?

_____

_____

_____

_____

2. The centuries-old patronage system that was in place during New Testament times sheds light on the word *charis*. What could a client do if they were in desperate need of financial help?

_____

_____

_____

_____

_____

_____

_____

3. How was the word *charis* used within the patronage system?

_____

_____

_____

_____

_____

_____

4. Who was a *sectorem*, and what role could they play if a client did not know any potential patrons? What must the broker do in order to help the client?

_____

_____

_____

_____

_____

_____

5. What kind of repayment strings were attached to the undeserved *charis* gift that the patron was willing to give to the client? How surprising is that? What was expected of the client?

_____

_____

_____

_____

_____

6. Based upon this life-changing gift that was free and undeserved, how did the extension of this *charis* create an ongoing connection between the two parties (and broker, if involved)?

_____

_____

_____

_____

_____

7. Does the paraphrase of Ephesians 2:8–9 that incorporates these concepts help give you a new understanding of *charis* as undeserved? How so?

_____

_____

_____

_____

8. Describe how Jesus played the role of *sectorem* and how that paints a beautiful picture of what God has done for us.

_____

_____

_____

_____

9. In what amazing way does the biblical patron-broker-client model differ from the Greek/Roman model? How was this first seen in the Garden of Eden?

_____

_____

_____

_____

10. In Luke 19:10, Jesus says the Son of Man came "to seek and to save that which was lost." How does this differ from what any wealthy patron or broker in Rome would ever have done?

_____

_____

_____

_____

11. Take some time to reflect on our desperate need of God's generosity as stated in Ephesians 2:4–5. What has His *charis* done for us?

_____

_____

_____

_____

12. What is stated in Romans 5:6–8 that leaves no doubt as to whether God's grace is wholly unmerited and completely undeserved? Have you recognized this to be true in your life? In what ways have you, and in what ways have you not?

_____

_____

_____

_____

13. Having received *charis*, how should you live the rest of your life?

_____

_____

_____

_____

_____

CHAPTER 5

AMAZINGLY UNEARNED

1. Have you ever received a birthday present from a friend who, upon seeing your delight in opening it, told you what you owed them for your gift? When is a gift not a gift?

_____

_____

_____

_____

2. Authentic, biblical grace is unearned. What is the relationship between grace and our sins and sinfulness?

_____

_____

_____

_____

3. What is the relationship between the first Adam and the second? How have we added to our debt inherited from Adam, and how have we contributed to the debt cancellation?

_____

_____

_____

_____

_____

4. According to Colossians 2:13–14, what is the only way to cancel the record of debt that stood against us? What is God saying to you about your debt?

_____

_____

_____

_____

_____

5. What powerful lesson can you take from Dr. E. V. Hill's story?

_____

_____

_____

_____

_____

6. Have you experienced a situation where you *knew* that it was God who provided for your need? Describe it.

_____

_____

_____

_____

_____

7. Read John 19:29–30. When Jesus shouted *Tetelestai!* from the cross, how was that word understood in the ancient Greek-speaking world?

_____

_____

_____

_____

8. Do you believe that your debt of sins has been stamped PAID IN FULL and nailed to the cross? Every sin, from the smallest to the biggest? Where do you need to get in agreement with God and start believing this is true for you?

_____

_____

_____

_____

9. In the light of *tetelestai*, describe how insulting it must be to God when we try to earn, merit, or pay for the forgiveness of our sins.

_____

_____

_____

_____

10. Describe some of the ways, subtle and not so subtle, you have tried to earn or merit God's approval and favor.

_____

_____

_____

_____

_____

11. How did Dick and Rick Hoyt personify a picture of grace? Where are you in that picture?

_____

_____

_____

_____

12. Write a declaration about God's grace based upon what you have learned from Colossians 2:13–14 and John 19:29–30.

_____

_____

_____

_____

_____

_____

CHAPTER 6

AMAZINGLY IMMUTABLE

1. One of the key attributes of our heavenly Father is His *immutability*. What is the meaning of the Greek word *ametathetos* that is used twice in Hebrews 6:17–18? What does that tell you about God's character?

_____

_____

_____

_____

2. From the following verses, write down what you think is the key declaration:

Numbers 23:19—

_____

1 Samuel 15:29—

_____

Malachi 3:6—

_____

Titus 1:2—

_____

3. The fact that God cannot change is an important, comforting truth, but what happens to many believers' understanding of grace as they live the Christian life? What paradigm shift is made as reflected in the Disneyland ticket-book system?

_____

_____

_____

_____

_____

4. How does Colossians 2:6 in tandem with Ephesians 2:8–9 refute that paradigm shift?

_____

_____

_____

_____

_____

5. Describe how Colossians 2:7 makes this even clearer, especially when it is based on the patron-client system through which the Greek concept of *charis* originated.

_____

_____

_____

_____

6. What danger does Paul note in Colossians 2:8–10 that will move us out of the humble position that salvation is a gift? What is the truth about our relationship with Jesus?

_____

_____

_____

_____

7. The entire book of Galatians is a letter from Paul to a group of people who were being seduced away from grace and back into the lifeless system of rule following, law keeping, and trying to pay back. Write your own paraphrase of Galatians 3:1–5.

_____

_____

_____

_____

8. Why does Paul give the Galatians such a stern warning? What foundational truth was being lost?

_____

_____

_____

_____

_____

9. What was Paul's prescription to cure this wandering away from God's gracious system? What contrast does he express here?

_____

_____

_____

_____

_____

10. If the Galatians were to fully fall back into the fruitless, frustrating system of trying to merit, deserve, and earn, what was Paul's grim diagnosis? What did he mean?

_____

_____

_____

_____

_____

11. Have you ever found yourself wandering down the same path as the Galatians? Describe your experience. Where did you end up?

_____

_____

_____

_____

12. When we say that this new system established and sealed by the blood of Jesus through His sacrificial death on the cross is literally a _new covenant_, how is this distinct from the Old Covenant?

_____

_____

_____

_____

_____

13. Reread and revisit your thoughts on Hebrews 6:17–18. What powerful position do the "heirs of promise" hold? Do you think of yourself as an heir of promise?

_____

_____

_____

_____

14. What "hope" is the writer of Hebrews referring to in Hebrews 6:19? How does this become an anchor for our soul?

_____

_____

_____

_____

_____

15. How was this message a special comfort to the recipients of the book of Hebrews?

_____

_____

_____

_____

_____

16. After what you've learned so far, do you understand Paul's exasperation in Galatians 3:3? If Paul were here today, what do you think he would say to you as a summary of his thoughts on the New Covenant?

_____

_____

_____

_____

_____

PART 2

NEW AND BETTER, PERIOD.

CHAPTER 7

A NEW AND BETTER COVENANT

1. With accumulated centuries of poring over the Law and the Prophets, what did the Jewish religious authorities expect about the Messiah? What did none of them expect the Messiah to do that Jesus did?

_____

_____

_____

_____

2. Why should these authorities have thoroughly understood a new covenant? Approximately when was Jeremiah 31:31–34 written? Beyond the promise of a new covenant, what did God say it would be?

_____

_____

_____

_____

3. Why does God choose to operate through covenant agreements with us? What do covenants establish?

_____

_____

_____

_____

_____

4. God picked Moses to be the mediator of His covenant with the Israelites. He also picked a form of covenant that they, especially Moses, a prince of Egypt, would have already been familiar with, a suzerain-vassal treaty. Describe this type of treaty.

_____

_____

_____

_____

_____

5. How is a parity covenant different? What is involved between the two parties, what does that signify, what declaration is made, and how is it sealed?

_____

_____

_____

_____

_____

6. Why did God choose the suzerain-vassal model as the form of His covenant with the Israelites? What are the short and long versions of that covenant?

_____

_____

_____

_____

_____

7. At that point in redemptive history, why was a peer-to-peer treaty not possible?

_____

_____

_____

_____

_____

8. What does it mean that the suzerain-vassal form of covenant was a _conditional_ agreement? Is that how the Old Covenant was stated? Give a biblical example of this.

_____

_____

_____

_____

_____

9. What does the "if…then" aspect allow for that leads to Jeremiah's prophecy?

_____

_____

_____

_____

_____

10. Who is the mediator of the New Covenant, and what does Hebrews 8:6–7 tell us about this New Covenant?

_____

_____

_____

_____

_____

11. In Hebrews 8:8–12, the writer quotes all of Jeremiah 31:31–34. Does this leave any room for disputing the legitimacy of the New Covenant? What good news docs this hold for you?

_____

_____

_____

_____

_____

12. What is the Holy Spirit saying to you about this chapter? Take a moment and write down what He says.

CHAPTER 8

NEW AND BETTER VERSUS OBSOLETE AND VANISHING

1. What does it mean that the book of Hebrews was written in an in-between time? To whom was it written, by whom, and by the time it was written, what major events had happened with the Church?

_____

_____

_____

_____

2. In Luke 24:44–45, what message did the risen Jesus give to His disciples to take to the world? As they went out, where was their first stop?

_____

_____

_____

3. Congregations of believing Jews sprang up everywhere, with some who had not yet fully committed. Why would many Jews be reluctant to embrace Jesus as Messiah? For any Jewish person thinking about professing faith in Jesus Christ, what might it cost them?

_____

_____

_____

_____

4. Given what the Hebrews faced, explain the importance of the exhortation in Hebrews 10:24–25. What "Day" is the writer talking about?

_____

_____

_____

_____

5. In Hebrews 4:1–2, what dire warnings are given to Jewish readers who were hanging around the fringes of the Jesus people assemblies but hadn't yet committed and surrendered? What was going on in the overlap period that was a problem for many Jesus followers?

_____

_____

_____

_____

6. At the time of the writing of Hebrews, what momentous event was only four or five years ahead for the city of Jerusalem? Before the Romans finished, what was completely and utterly fulfilled?

_____

_____

_____

_____

_____

7. What became of the Old Covenant system of 613 laws and regulations and all of the Temple rites and rituals and religious hierarchy?

_____

_____

_____

_____

_____

_____

8. When was the Old Covenant enacted and culminated?

_____

_____

_____

_____

_____

9. When was the New Covenant enacted and culminated?

_____

_____

_____

_____

10. What contrast is made between what the Old Covenant was written upon versus the New Covenant?

_____

_____

_____

_____

_____

11. If the writer of Hebrews had not made his point clear enough, what bombshell does he drop in Hebrews 8:13? When did this happen? So why did it linger?

_____

_____

_____

_____

_____

12. Have you been slow to fully embrace all that Jesus brings with Him in the New Covenant? If so, what's holding you back? What change in your thinking will help you improve in this area?

_____

_____

_____

_____

_____

_____

CHAPTER 9

WHY A NEW COVENANT?

1. When you hear the word *upgrade*, what is your immediate thought? What would you like to upgrade?

_____

_____

_____

_____

_____

2. How can a God who does all things perfectly upgrade a covenant system that He put in place?

_____

_____

_____

_____

_____

3. Jesus ushered in a *new* and *better* covenant than the one established with the Israelites through Moses. A different *kind* of covenant. Write a summary of the suzerain-vassal model upon which the original covenant was built.

_____

_____

_____

_____

_____

4. Write a summary of the parity covenant that was the model for the New Covenant.

_____

_____

_____

_____

_____

5. Why was it not possible to institute a parity covenant mediated by Moses in his day?

_____

_____

_____

_____

_____

6. What was God's plan from the very beginning, from the very day of the fall of mankind in the Garden of Eden, for restoring us to intimate fellowship with Him? How did the Old Covenant figure into this plan?

_____

_____

_____

_____

7. Though intentionally vague, immediately after God pronounced the terrible implications of what Adam and Eve had done, what remarkable promise did He make in Genesis 3:15? Who was the "Descendant"?

_____

_____

_____

_____

8. As the mediator of the new and better covenant, who did Jesus represent and who was this covenant between? How is it possible for us to be included in such a covenant?

_____

_____

_____

_____

9. Through the miracle of the new birth, what do Galatians 3:27, Romans 6:3, and 1 Corinthians 12:13 tell us happens when we are baptized into Jesus? How have you found this principle to be true in your life?

_____

_____

_____

_____

_____

10. Describe what it means when we say the first covenant was a necessary bridge to the New Covenant. What purpose did Abraham, the chosen people, and the Old Covenant serve?

_____

_____

_____

_____

_____

11. Read Genesis 22:1–19 about how God asked Abraham to sacrifice his only, miraculously conceived son. Why did God test Abraham's faith in _that_ way?

_____

_____

_____

_____

12. Spend some time meditating about the wonder of what God did through His covenants, and then write a prayer to the Lord, telling Him how you feel.

_____

_____

_____

_____

_____

_____

CHAPTER 10

BY GRACE: A BETTER HUSBAND

1. Every person ever born was, or still is, "married" to someone...or more accurately some*thing*. Who is every believer married to, according to Revelation 21:9 and Ephesians 5:32? Do you consider this true for you?

_____

_____

_____

_____

_____

2. Less well known, what does Paul state in Romans 7:1–4 is a *second marriage* for all believers? Why was it so confusing for the thousands of Gentile converts to the Jesus movement to understand and relate to the Old Testament Law versus grace?

_____

_____

_____

_____

_____

_____

3. In the first five chapters of Romans, what did Paul make clear is the only thing that qualifies us to be connected to God? Who does Romans 4:3 state is the great example of this? Based on this, what does Paul state boldly about grace in Romans 6:14?

_____

_____

_____

_____

_____

4. It wasn't just the Israelites who were "married" to the Law. According to Romans 1:17–20, what holds all of humanity accountable to God's perfect and eternal standards of holiness and purity? What does that mean?

_____

_____

_____

_____

_____

5. What is the only way for us to be released from our marriage to the Law? How is this explicitly stated in Romans 6:3–4?

_____

_____

_____

_____

_____

6. Beyond being released from the Law, what does Romans 7:4 state happens?

_____

_____

_____

_____

_____

_____

7. Our ex-husband, the Law, was perfect, but it was inadequate. How was it inadequate, and what *was* and *is* the Law's job?

_____

_____

_____

_____

_____

8. What kind of husband does the Law make, and who is our upgrade? As reborn believers, why would we want to go back to our ex? What is always the outcome?

_____

_____

_____

_____

_____

9. When we say, "The Law cannot justify," what does that mean? Write the phrases from Romans 3:10–11, 20, and 28 that make this clear.

_____

_____

_____

_____

_____

10. The justification we so desperately require comes only by grace through faith in the Lord Jesus Christ. What stands out to you in _The Message_'s paraphrase of Galatians 3:1–3 as effective to stop the people who were being seduced into going back to the Law?

_____

_____

_____

_____

11. Describe what is meant by the phrase, "The Law cannot empower you."

_____

_____

_____

_____

_____

12. Revisit Romans 7:4 and connect it with John 15:5. What vital truth does this tell you?

_____

_____

_____

_____

_____

13. "The Law can't make you righteous." How is this shown in Galatians 2:21 as well as made clear through Abraham's experience?

_____

_____

_____

_____

_____

14. Since the Father's goal from the very beginning was to restore us to Himself, why is righteousness a key, and what is the only way to righteousness?

_____

_____

_____

_____

_____

15. Do you find yourself behaving as if you're still married to the Law, still obligated to love, honor, and obey a list of rules and regulations? How so? Describe your experience.

_____

_____

_____

_____

_____

16. When you go back and start serving the Law again, what are you actually saying about your relation with your new and better husband, Jesus? Does that make any sense?

_____

_____

_____

_____

17. What makes the gospel such good news at this point? Write a bold declaration that this is true for you.

_____

_____

_____

_____

_____

_____

CHAPTER 11

BY GRACE: BETTER RIGHTEOUSNESS

1. Previous to the giving of the Sermon on the Mount, what does Matthew 9:35 tell us Jesus had been doing? What two main messages had He been proclaiming?

_____

_____

_____

_____

_____

2. What had John the Baptist's message been, and what pronouncements did it include?

_____

_____

_____

_____

3. After John was put in prison, Jesus took up His cousin's prophetic mantle, but with what two significant additions?

_____

_____

_____

_____

_____

4. Many of Jesus' parables about the coming kingdom were sorting and separating metaphors. What metaphors did He use, and what was He saying about the people who listened?

_____

_____

_____

_____

_____

5. How did Jesus' parables about the kingdom being "at hand," "near," and "upon you" suggest the opposite of the universal Jewish assumption about the kingdom?

_____

_____

_____

_____

_____

6. Among the hearers of the Sermon of the Mount were Pharisees, scribes, and other devout Jews who actually thought they were successfully keeping the Law in every aspect. Describe how the rich young ruler expressed this belief and how Jesus exposed his claim to perfect righteousness as a lie.

_____

_____

_____

_____

7. Many in the crowd at the Sermon on the Mount believed they had a form of righteousness. Piece by piece, how did Jesus dismantle their smug, self-satisfied belief in their Old Covenant righteousness? How did Matthew 5:22, 28, and 32 express the true meaning of these commandments? Why did He do it this way?

_____

_____

_____

_____

_____

8. In the Beatitudes, what kind of people does Jesus state will receive the kingdom? How are these people "blessed"?

_____

_____

_____

9. For the listeners who already thought they were righteous but were not actually hungering and thirsting for it, what bomb did Jesus drop on them in Matthew 5:20? Why should this have caused those people to despair?

_____

_____

_____

_____

10. On your best day of holy living, what would you list as the "dos" you accomplished and the "don'ts" you avoided? What does Jesus say to that? What does Isaiah 64:6 declare?

_____

_____

_____

_____

11. How did the Sermon on the Mount serve the same purpose as the Law? How does Hebrews 10:3–4 show the blood of animal sacrifices in the Old Covenant system as totally inadequate? How does James 2:10 crush any false, prideful faux-righteousness?

_____

_____

_____

_____

12. What is the only way to a right standing with God, and how do Isaiah 61:10, Galatians 3:27, and 2 Corinthians 5:21 describe this?

_____

_____

_____

_____

13. How is it possible that blood-washed believers are as welcome in God's presence as Jesus is? What message of hope do you feel God is personally speaking to your heart about through this?

_____

_____

_____

_____

14. Righteousness is an amazing gift, but how does it get even better? Read Romans 8:29. How have you seen this working in your life?

_____

_____

_____

_____

_____

15. We're not saved by good works, so what role do good works play? What clear message on the relationship of grace and good works is stated in Ephesians 2:8–10?

_____

_____

_____

_____

16. What transformations in our life only come as we experience God's presence—in intimate fellowship, conversation, and communion with Him?

_____

_____

_____

_____

17. Are shame and guilt keeping you out of God's presence? Don't wait another moment to receive the extraordinary gift of Jesus' righteousness, then declare His "right standing" with the Father as yours as well. Write a prayer of thanks for a righteousness infinitely better than anything we could ever produce on our own.

_____

_____

_____

_____

CHAPTER 12

BY GRACE: BETTER REST

1. How similar would you say your life as a Christian is to Martha's? Have the sins you've committed kept you from turning to God in prayer for help and comfort in times of need? Explain your thoughts.

_____

_____

_____

_____

2. Sins of omission reflect obligations that Christians often feel they must fulfill. Do you have a list of boxes to check to ensure God is pleased with you? What are they?

_____

_____

_____

_____

3. When some believers hear others talking about having a deep, satisfying, intimate relationship with God, how is Martha's response typical? Has this ever been your response?

_____

_____

_____

_____

4. Do you have assurance that the little child inside you was accepted and received and welcomed in God's lap, or do passages such as Psalm 51 keep you in fear that the day might come when God tires of your continual need of forgiveness and leaves you separated from His presence?

_____

_____

_____

_____

5. Describe how Mary's experience of the Christian life has been radically different from Martha's. What teachings helped her find a close, intimate, life-giving relationship with God?

_____

_____

_____

_____

6. How does what Martha believes, as well as what her teachers and mentors are telling her about graceless legalism, keep her trapped in the nightmare Paul describes in Romans 7:15?

_____

_____

_____

_____

_____

7. How does Romans 8:14–15 mark the distinction between Martha and Mary? What is the way to freedom?

_____

_____

_____

_____

_____

8. How does Hebrews 3 and 4 also model the distinction between Martha and Mary? What invitation does God give for the believer in the New Covenant?

_____

_____

_____

_____

_____

9. According to Hebrews 4:9–10, how do we fully enter into the rest that is gifted to us through what Jesus earned and deserved on our behalf?

_____

_____

_____

_____

_____

10. Having stepped into the Promised Land of living in Jesus' righteousness and qualification, what does 2 Corinthians 3:18 state is opened up to us?

_____

_____

_____

_____

_____

11. Imagine standing with the Israelites in the harsh, inhospitable desert looking into the Promised Land that was lush green, filled with abundance and bounty. What is the only remaining question before them? Is that where you are spiritually? Do you just need to lay down a pride-driven need to earn and deserve?

_____

_____

_____

_____

12. How do you join Mary and cross over the border?

_____

_____

_____

_____

_____

_____

CHAPTER 13

BY GRACE: BETTER WORKS

1. Stepping into the grace and rest of the New Covenant doesn't make your actions and choices irrelevant. But while Martha and Mary appear to be doing very similar works, Martha is left exhausted and feels far from God while Mary is generally at peace and enjoys near-constant communion with her heavenly Father. Why? Expand on your answer from your own experience with works.

_____

_____

_____

_____

_____

2. As a new creation in Christ, what were you designed to do? What did Jesus say about this in Matthew 5:16, and what did Paul state in Ephesians 2:8–9?

_____

_____

_____

_____

_____

3. How does the writer of Hebrews express his frustration with the recipients of his letter in Hebrews 5:11–12? What "elementary" principle of the faith is at the top of his list from which they should have already graduated? What does that mean? What were these new Jewish believers still trying to do?

_____

_____

_____

_____

_____

4. How do good works differ from dead works? What key does John 15:5 hold for our understanding?

_____

_____

_____

_____

_____

5. What will most certainly keep you in Jesus Kindergarten? When you enter into the Sabbath rest, what does that mean?

_____

_____

_____

_____

_____

6. Read the account in Genesis 15. Describe what was happening between God and Abraham.

_____

_____

_____

_____

_____

_____

7. What does all of this tell us about good works and our relationship with God? What does it save us from? Into what does it bring us?

_____

_____

_____

_____

_____

_____

8. When the Israelites crossed over into Canaan, which God described as entering into rest, they still had to defeat enemies, slay giants, and work their new farms. Why could God call this a form of rest?

_____

_____

_____

_____

9. How do 1 Peter 1:17, Matthew 16:27, and Revelation 22:12 show the importance of good works as opposed to dead works? What sense of expectancy should this build in us?

_____

_____

_____

_____

10. What rewards are earned by dead works? In Matthew 6:1–4, how did Jesus impress this fact upon the Pharisees, who were the kings of dead works?

_____

_____

_____

_____

11. What beautiful promise does Jesus give in Matthew 6:19–20? How can you use your understanding of grace to do good works and be more empowered to do good works?

_____

_____

_____

_____

_____

12. According to 1 John 2:28, what is the key to a lifestyle of laying up treasure in heaven? How can you be confident that at Jesus' return, this will be yours?

_____

_____

_____

_____

_____

13. In Jesus, we have a better husband, a better righteousness, a better rest, and better works that produce better rewards. Reflect upon what God is saying to you through this.

_____

_____

_____

_____

PART 3

SONS AND DAUGHTERS, PERIOD.

CHAPTER 14

A SHEPHERD. A SEARCHER. A FATHER.

1. Jesus got a lot of complaints. What complaint did the Pharisees and scribes make about Him in Luke 15:1–2? What was Jesus' previous response to the same complaint? How did He respond this time?

_____

_____

_____

_____

_____

2. Jesus ministered to three types of Jews living in Israel. Describe them.

_____

_____

_____

_____

3. Who constituted the group that the religious elite complained about the most? Why were they on Jesus' heart, and was His message any different to them than to the others?

_____

_____

_____

_____

_____

4. Read Luke 15:4–7. What does the shepherd do, and how does He make sure that His complainers understand this parable? How does this parable align with Jesus' statement in Matthew 15:24?

_____

_____

_____

_____

_____

5. What was Jesus' mission before He laid down His life on the cross? What prophetic role was He playing?

_____

_____

_____

_____

_____

6. Read Luke 15:8–10. What does the woman's frantic search for the coin tell you, and what is the result? Take a moment and reflect on the joy of heaven. How amazing must that be?

_____

_____

_____

_____

7. It is the *repentance* that produces the rejoicing in heaven. Jesus' willingness to associate with sinners is used by some as a sort of endorsement of accepting and approving of sinful lifestyles and choices and as a club with which to beat believers who stand against harmful cultural trends. How is that not true and a false narrative about believers?

_____

_____

_____

_____

8. Who do you think Jesus had in mind when His first parable featured a shepherd? How did He come and find you and bring you safely home?

_____

_____

_____

_____

9. Write down some of the biblical reasons why the woman searching for her lost key may represent the Holy Spirit. How did the Holy Spirit come searching for you?

_____

_____

_____

_____

_____

_____

10. Read Luke 15:11–32. Surely the father with the broken heart depicts God the Father. What message does this bring you about what lies at the heart of the divine Trinity?

_____

_____

_____

_____

_____

_____

CHAPTER 15

TWO SONS. ONE PROBLEM.

1. The parable of the prodigal son is the third parable in a row given as both an answer and a rebuke to the critical Pharisees and scribes who didn't like Jesus' habit of engaging with people who had abandoned the Jewish system of works. How is a large, working cattle ranch similar to the situation Jesus envisions here with the father's estate?

_____

_____

_____

_____

2. Describe what it meant for the younger son to ask for his share of his father's estate.

_____

_____

_____

3. How does the father respond? How much do each of the brothers receive? What is the significance of the Greek word translated "livelihood"?

_____

_____

_____

_____

_____

_____

4. What did the prodigal leave behind, and where did he end up?

_____

_____

_____

_____

_____

_____

5. When he came to his senses, what did he realize and determine to do? What did he assume his place would be?

_____

_____

_____

_____

_____

_____

6. Write a summary of how the father reacts to his son's return, keeping in mind that this is a description of God's Father-heart.

_____

_____

_____

_____

_____

7. Write a summary of how the older brother reacts to his brother's return, keeping in mind that this is a description of those who were committed to trying to remain faithful to the Old Covenant rules and regulations.

_____

_____

_____

_____

_____

8. In what way did the younger son misunderstand his position with his father?

_____

_____

_____

_____

_____

9. In what way did the older son misunderstand his position with his father? How does he state this in his own words?

_____

_____

_____

_____

_____

10. What was already available to the older son? How was continuing to operate as a hired hand an insult to his father?

_____

_____

_____

_____

_____

_____

11. What immediate meaning of the "prodigal" parable would have been clear to everyone who heard Jesus speak it?

_____

_____

_____

_____

_____

12. What would Jesus' listeners also have understood He was saying through the example of the angry, resentful older brother? Of what had they convinced themselves?

_____

_____

_____

_____

_____

13. How had the Pharisees failed to understand the heart of God and His core reason for entering into covenant with them? And how is that reflected in their response to Jesus all along?

_____

_____

_____

_____

_____

14. At this point, do you identify more with the prodigal or the older brother? Take some time and write an honest answer.

_____

_____

_____

_____

_____

CHAPTER 16

YOUR ROBE

1. One of the many fascinating themes and threads in the Bible is robes. Think about all the places robes or body-covering garments appear in the amazing storyline of Scripture. Describe the first robe, who made it, and why.

_____

_____

_____

_____

2. In the ancient world of the Bible, robes designated status and authority. Joseph's robe may be the most famous. Describe it and the status it designated.

_____

_____

_____

_____

3. Describe what the High Priest was to wear as he ministered in the Holy Place and especially in the Most Holy Place, also known as the Holy of Holies. How did the Holy of Holies re-create the setting of Adam back in the Garden of Eden?

_____

_____

_____

_____

_____

4. What powerful lesson is shown when once each year, the High Priest would enter into the Holy of Holies, into God's presence? What assurance and hope does this give you?

_____

_____

_____

_____

_____

5. Read 1 Samuel 18:1–3. What does this robe signify?

_____

_____

_____

_____

6. Read John 19. Describe the significance of the robe Jesus was wearing the night He was arrested.

_____

_____

_____

_____

_____

7. In the light of the significance of the previous robes mentioned, what does the fact that Jesus was stripped of everything on the cross mean? Take some time to reflect on the wonder of what He did, then write a prayer of thanks.

_____

_____

_____

_____

_____

8. In the prodigal's return to his father, what did he believe? To receive what he hoped for, what was he convinced he must do?

_____

_____

_____

_____

9. Revisit and summarize what we have discovered about God's grace-gifts. In what ways will grasping this truth change everything about your life going forward?

_____

_____

_____

_____

10. Clearly, the prodigal had been arrogant, foolish, sinful, and depraved, doing nothing to earn the three gifts his father gave him upon his return. What do the words "I am no longer worthy to be called your son" imply? What does this reveal?

_____

_____

_____

_____

11. How do we, as beloved sons and daughters of a gracious heavenly Father, bring this same mindset into church on the weekend? Use the example in the book if it fits you, or write your own.

_____

_____

_____

_____

12. What is the problem with believing that your standing with God is in any way related to your performance? How deeply ingrained in you do you think this is?

_____

_____

_____

_____

_____

13. In Isaiah 61:10, what did Isaiah foresee, and how does the High Priest's robe of linen depict what the ultimate High Priest, Jesus, has done?

_____

_____

_____

_____

_____

14. Read Zechariah 3:3–4 as well as 1 Samuel 2–3. What did Zechariah see, and how did this relate to the history of the priesthood in Israel over the centuries?

_____

_____

_____

_____

15. What brings a change to this robe, and who bestows it? What good news can you take from this?

_____

_____

_____

_____

_____

16. Who else is present in that scene, and what do you need to understand about him? Are you aware that he is the source of the shame and condemnation we so often feel?

_____

_____

_____

_____

_____

17. In the presence of the critical, accusatory Pharisees, why did Jesus choose a robe as the first gift from the father to the prodigal son? What did it also look forward to in a soon-coming day?

_____

_____

_____

_____

_____

18. Based on Romans 3:22–24, where does righteousness come from, how does it come, and by what are we "justified freely"? As if that was not clear enough, what two things does Paul state in Romans 5:17 that we received through Christ?

_____

_____

_____

_____

19. Have you realized that when you were wrapped in Jesus' righteousness, not only were you forgiven and justified, but you were also freed from shame and guilt? What profound difference does this understanding make upon how you live out your relationship with Jesus?

_____

_____

_____

_____

20. Because many believers are sin-conscious rather than gift-of-righteousness-conscious, they continue to use their amazing grace-gift of access to God sporadically and sheepishly. What do Ephesians 3:11–12 and Hebrews 4:15–16 tell us about the power of Jesus' blood in the New Covenant?

_____

_____

_____

_____

_____

_____

21. Embracing and internalizing your true identity as a son or daughter of God, rather than the false identity of a servant, doesn't just happen instantly. What is the secret to the process?

_____

_____

_____

_____

_____

_____

CHAPTER 17

YOUR RING

1. Describe what a signet ring was and what it did.

_____

_____

_____

_____

_____

2. What did the signet ring given to Joseph in Genesis 41:42–43 and the ring given to Haman in Esther 3:10 convey?

_____

_____

_____

_____

_____

3. Centuries later, in Jesus' day, wealthy Jewish fathers were still using signet rings. When the prodigal's father put the ring on his hand, what was he giving this son?

_____

_____

_____

_____

4. Being a God of order, hierarchy, and process, God works through delegated authority. To whom did He originally delegate authority over Planet Earth, and to whom does Jesus suggest that authority was forfeited via Adam's fall? What is meant by an *archon* of the *kosmos*?

_____

_____

_____

_____

5. What does the second temptation of Jesus in Luke 4:5–8 and the statement "all this authority" suggest about the rulership of the world?

_____

_____

_____

6. In a very real sense, God designated Adam as His official *archon* for Planet Earth, legally and covenantally delegating His sovereign authority to man. When Adam fell, what became of the covenant, and who alone can recover what was legally lost?

_____

_____

_____

_____

7. What statement in John 14:30 is the key to that recovery of delegated authority?

_____

_____

_____

_____

8. What does Jesus' statement in Matthew 28:18–19 declare has changed after His resurrection and victory over death? How does Paul state that Jesus disarmed the principalities and powers? What is the significance of the meaning of *apekduomai*?

_____

_____

_____

_____

9. What power did Satan retain after being stripped of authority? What does he intend for us to do as he did with Eve?

_____

_____

_____

_____

10. As the Last Adam, what was Jesus saying He had regained? With this in mind, what did Paul pray for in Ephesians 1:19–23? The verses in this prayer speak of what? What is the significance of the Greek word translated "power" in the passage?

_____

_____

_____

_____

11. Take the time to read Matthew 16:19, Mark 16:17, Luke 9:1 and 10:18–19, John 14:12, 2 Corinthians 10:2–5, Ephesians 2:6, and 1 John 4:4. What do these verses tell us about our authority as born-again believers?

_____

_____

_____

_____

12. So why did Jesus have the father of the prodigal place a ring on his finger in His parable?

_____

_____

_____

_____

_____

13. What does Jesus state about delegated authority in Matthew 28:18–20? How does that restore God's original marching orders to Adam and Eve as well as His order to the Israelites to enter the Land of Promise?

_____

_____

_____

_____

_____

14. What is the mind-blowing aspect of this revelation? How is that reflected in Matthew 6:10 and John 14:12?

_____

_____

_____

_____

_____

15. When you and I, as prodigals, returned to a relationship with our heavenly Father, the ring He placed on our fingers is a ring of authority. It has two names on it: your name and Jesus Christ, King of Kings. At what level would you say that you are walking in this delegated authority?

_____

_____

_____

_____

_____

_____

CHAPTER 18

KEYS TO WEARING THE RING

1. Jesus declared that He'd received "all authority...in heaven and on earth" (Matthew 28:18). He also said He was delegating to His followers "the authority to tread on serpents and scorpions, and over all the power of the enemy" and that "nothing shall by any means hurt" us (Luke 10:19). Throughout the Bible, serpents and scorpions are symbols for demonic powers. So why do you think so many Christians are not walking in complete victory over the enemy?

_____

_____

_____

_____

_____

_____

_____

2. What is the first common characteristic of those who wear and wield their ring of authority? How could that have kept the prodigal from being ushered back into his father's grand house?

_____

_____

_____

_____

3. Jesus had gifted seventy of His disciples the power over the enemy. In Luke 10:20–21, Jesus first reveals that the source of their authority is that they belong to the kingdom of God. What causes pure, Holy Spirit joy to overflow out of Jesus in an eruption of prophetic prayer?

_____

_____

_____

_____

4. But immediately after confirming that He had indeed gifted His own authority to them, what does Jesus caution them about here? How is this also a reminder to rightly understand spiritual cause and effect?

_____

_____

_____

_____

5. Read James 4:6. What does the contrast between grace and pride tell you? Use the analogy of the sailboat.

_____

_____

_____

_____

_____

6. In the personal story of the woman who was under demonic influence, what made the humble little grandmother effective? What will pride do in a situation such as that?

_____

_____

_____

_____

_____

7. Have you ever experienced a situation where pride kept you from exercising your authority as a representative of God's kingdom to push back darkness and bring redemptive hope? Describe it.

_____

_____

_____

_____

8. What is the second key to the authority Jesus has given us? Most believers are not even aware of what? What was Jesus saying to His disciples in Mark 4:40?

_____

_____

_____

_____

9. It is one thing to possess authority. It is another thing to know it and wield it. What type of faith was demonstrated in Matthew 9:18–26 and John 11:3?

_____

_____

_____

_____

10. In Matthew 8:5–10, what was it about the centurion's faith that caused Jesus to "marvel"? What did the centurion understand about delegated authority? How does that make for a "great faith" versus what Jesus was accustomed to in others?

_____

_____

_____

_____

11. What two things undermine our faith, or confident belief, in the authority Jesus has delegated to us? Write down a personal example of how your faith has been undermined by each one.

_____

_____

_____

_____

12. Faith, or *belief in the truth*, is a major key to exercising the authority we've been gifted by the Father in Jesus. What is the difference between unbelief and *mis-belief*? What is the meaning of the Greek word translated "truth" in John 8:32? Why does that make believing so powerful?

_____

_____

_____

_____

13. It is normal and common for the enemy to war against believers, but what lie must we not accept as normal? What other lie must we not accept about it? Give some biblical examples.

_____

_____

_____

_____

14. According to John 16:13, what is one of the vital ministries of the Holy Spirit? Give an example of when the Holy Spirit helped you apply the power of faith to a falsehood. What was the outcome?

_____

_____

_____

_____

15. Read Ephesians 6:10–20. The shield of faith is used for what? How do you wield it in battle? Describe one example from your experience when you did so.

_____

_____

_____

_____

_____

16. The third key to effectively walk in the authority Jesus delegated to us is *consecration*. What does that mean? What key to this is found in Romans 8:14?

_____

_____

_____

17. Why does a lack of surrender to God make it difficult to walk in authority?

_____

_____

_____

_____

_____

18. What vital lesson for victory over the devil can you take from the two main thoughts connected in James 4:6–7?

_____

_____

_____

_____

_____

19. How does grace remain the answer to everything about your life in God, including your authority? What assurance and hope does this give you?

_____

_____

_____

_____

_____

CHAPTER 19

YOUR SHOES

1. The Bible contains many significant references to shoes, and if you examine all those references as a whole, you start to get the impression that shoes have symbolic meaning. What instructions are we given about shoes/sandals in the following verses?

Exodus 3:5—

_____

Joshua 5:15—

_____

John 1:27—

_____

Ephesians 6:15—

_____

Luke 15:22—

_____

2. In the Scriptures, shoes represent *rights*, so it follows that the act of taking off shoes signifies the surrendering of rights. When it comes to seeing this in the Old Testament, what is the key to reading it? To whom does everything in the Old Testament point?

_____

_____

_____

_____

3. Read Ruth 4 from the perspective that it is one of the most beautiful and moving types and foreshadowings of what Jesus did for us. Who was Ruth, and what was she doing? Who was Boaz, and what was his relationship to Naomi, Ruth's mother-in-law?

_____

_____

_____

_____

4. Why was the kinsman-redeemer right established, and to whom did the responsibility to redeem ordinarily belong? For Boaz to redeem the land that originally belonged to Ruth's late husband, what was required, and what was the problem?

_____

_____

_____

5. What ceremony was involved for the kinsman-redeemer to step into his role? What did that act signify?

_____

_____

_____

_____

_____

6. Looking back to how Moses (Exodus 3:5) and Joshua (Joshua 5:15) were commanded to remove their shoes, what were they needing to do? When we encounter Jesus, what is the question?

_____

_____

_____

_____

7. What does the New Covenant make us into that the Old Covenant could not?

_____

_____

_____

_____

_____

8. Back to the parable of the prodigal. If taking off your shoes means giving up your rights, what did it mean for the father to call for shoes to be placed on his son's feet?

_____

_____

_____

_____

_____

_____

9. Using the analogy of the shoes, what are we doing when we come to Jesus for salvation?

_____

_____

_____

_____

_____

_____

CHAPTER 20

WALKING IN YOUR RIGHTS AS SONS AND DAUGHTERS

1. What are the rights and privileges of sonship based upon in human families as well as God's family?

_____

_____

_____

_____

2. What privilege does 2 Chronicles 7:14 tell us is ours as those who have the shoes of sonship placed on our feet? If you were an orphan, what would this privilege mean to you?

_____

_____

_____

3. Another right that comes with those shoes is *access* to the Father that servants simply don't enjoy. How was that demonstrated in the story of the foreman who called the owner of the company "Mr. Big"?

_____

_____

_____

_____

4. How great a privilege is it to be able to call the God of the universe Dad? What do others call Him?

_____

_____

_____

_____

5. Take some time to meditate on Romans 8:15–16. What is God showing you about Himself and the role of the Holy Spirit in your life?

_____

_____

_____

_____

6. Based upon Ephesians 2:18 and 3:12, and Hebrews 4:16 and 10:19–22, describe the exact terms upon which we enjoy the right of free access to the Father and what that includes.

_____

_____

_____

_____

7. As with the symbol of the ring, how does Luke 10:19 show that the gift of the shoes of sonship confers a right to authority and power? Visualize you doing exactly that. What encouragement does this give you?

_____

_____

_____

_____

8. What do Psalm 110:1 and its reference in Hebrews 10:12–13 state Jesus' position is today? Who constitutes His body, and how are His enemies made a footstool? According to Ephesians 6:12, who is that enemy?

_____

_____

_____

9. According to Ephesians 6:15, what else do the shoes confer? What is the source of that empowering work?

_____

_____

_____

_____

_____

10. Read 2 Chronicles 28:1–15. What did the taking away and the restoring of the shoes of the captives mean? What does Paul tell us in Galatians 5:1?

_____

_____

_____

_____

_____

11. One way in which believers unnecessarily surrender their freedom is to go back into bondage to sin. How does this happen, and how is it described in Romans 6:15–23?

_____

_____

_____

_____

12. The second way we can surrender our freedom is to voluntarily go back into servitude to the Law. Describe how we let this happen and where we end up.

_____

_____

_____

_____

13. Read Galatians 4:21–26. What metaphor is Paul using for living under Old Covenant Law rather than under New Covenant grace? Describe the difference between the two sons who were born to Abraham.

_____

_____

_____

_____

14. What is Paul telling any Galatian believer who was being persuaded to follow pieces of the Law? What freedoms do we receive as a gift of sonship?

_____

_____

_____

_____

15. What good news can you take from this chapter to help you keep walking in freedom?

_____

_____

_____

_____

_____

_____

CHAPTER 21

SONS AND DAUGHTERS NOT SERVANTS

1. What does the word *parable* mean?

_____

_____

_____

_____

_____

2. In the case of the older brother in the parable of the prodigal son, what truth was Jesus using to expose the misconception of the scribes and Pharisees?

_____

_____

_____

_____

_____

3. What does the older brother tell you about the constant pull that we believers face? Give examples from your own experience.

_____

_____

_____

_____

_____

4. What does the "again" in Romans 8:15–16 tell you about living in the bondage of fear and shame?

_____

_____

_____

_____

_____

5. We *come* to Jesus as the prodigal in the story, yet it's possible to *live* in Jesus as the older brother. What had the older brother forfeited that was his by right of birth? How can you *serve* but not be a *servant*?

_____

_____

_____

_____

_____

6. What made the older son so angry? What was he showing about his status with his father in Luke 15:28–30?

_____

_____

_____

_____

_____

7. What happens the moment we start defining ourselves—our lives in God—in terms of what we do and don't do?

_____

_____

_____

_____

_____

8. Describe what is meant by an orphan spirit. The moment we are born again, what is the cry of our heart through the "spirit of adoption"? Over time, what can happen to that heart cry?

_____

_____

_____

_____

_____

9. Read Genesis 2:8–17. How does the metaphor of these two trees describe what too often happens to believers?

_____

_____

_____

_____

_____

10. Why must the orphan constantly work and strive to earn a place at the table? What is the greatest invitation ever offered that comes from the Father to the orphaned children of Adam?

_____

_____

_____

_____

_____

11. Have you found that it is so easy to become fixated on not becoming the prodigal—rebellious, sinful, and out of control—that you've allowed yourself to become the older brother? If so, explain your answer.

_____

_____

_____

_____

12. The older brother had already been given his legal portion of his father's estate. How does that make his statement in Luke 15:29 a lie, a false accusation of not being generous? What was he still thinking about his father?

_____

_____

_____

_____

13. It's easy to see the older brother's faulty thinking. Describe how we do the same with our heavenly Father.

_____

_____

_____

_____

_____

14. In Luke 15:31–32, what was the father's extraordinary first response to his son's angry outburst? What does the Greek word *teknon* connote here? How does it defeat the thought that we've done too much wrong and disqualified ourselves as children of the Father?

_____

_____

_____

_____

15. What follows that affectionate reaffirmation of identity is a reminder of the greatest sonship blessing of all. What is it? How was the older son afforded a privilege every servant on the estate would have given anything to enjoy?

_____

_____

_____

_____

_____

16. As a *teknon* of a gracious, generous Father, what does Hebrews 10:19–22 tell us about the new and living way into the Father's most intimate presence?

_____

_____

_____

_____

_____

17. How is that "Grace, Period"? What happens when we understand it?

_____

_____

_____

_____

_____

18. What does Jesus have the father in His parable cite as a second blessing of sonship? How is this saying what we saw previously in the parity covenant? What does it mean for you as one who is legally and spiritually in Christ?

_____

_____

_____

_____

_____

19. Given that legal and spiritual foundation, what mind-blowing statements does Jesus make in John 14:13, 15:7, and 16:15 to all those who follow Him?

_____

_____

_____

_____

_____

20. One of the most prominent and defining characteristics of our heavenly Father is generosity. Why do some believers never feel free to be generous? If you believe 2 Peter 1:3, how will that reality transform your living and giving?

_____

_____

_____

_____

21. Would you say that you have a scarcity mindset? In what ways? Write a prayer to the Lord telling Him how you feel as you reflect on this.

_____

_____

_____

_____

_____

22. Where will a hired-hand mentality keep you?

_____

_____

_____

_____

_____

23. In Jesus, we are not servants, even though we happily serve. We are beloved sons and daughters. And of us, the Father says today, "You are always with me. And everything I have is yours." Reflect upon how you can start to live by this amazing gift of grace every day.

_____

_____

_____

_____

_____

YES, IT'S GRACE . . . PERIOD.

1. The unveiling of the wonders of God's amazing grace may have initially sounded too good to be true, but hopefully this good news has rung a bell in your deepest heart. For many who don't know how to receive a gift, it really does seem impossible that God's offer of eternal relationship and connection could require nothing more than being humble enough to say yes to it. Or that we continue our lives in God the same way we began them. If you felt this way at the start of the book, has your view changed? In what ways?

_____

_____

_____

_____

_____

_____

2. For others, however, fear keeps them from embracing the full implications of divine grace. Fear of *what*?

_____

_____

_____

_____

3. Why do many well-intentioned pastors get nervous when someone preaches the g-word to their congregations without heaping portions of *but*s and *however*s and *on the other hand*s and *two oars* and other disclaimers to water down the stunning implications of the New Covenant? What do they regard as dangerous about it?

_____

_____

_____

_____

4. That grace does not produce sin but rather produces righteousness may seem totally counterintuitive. But explain how that is true in the way the Law and grace present a paradox.

_____

_____

_____

_____

5. The Law is built on fear while grace is built on love. Describe how love is the strongest force for personal change and transformation in the universe.

_____

_____

_____

_____

_____

6. In contrast with love, how does the Law actually pull us in the opposite direction? As a reflection of God's perfection and holiness, what is the purpose of the Law?

_____

_____

_____

_____

_____

7. What does 2 Corinthians 3:18 tell us is the surest, highest source of transformation? Which makes you more likely to enter into this—the Law or grace?

_____

_____

_____

_____

_____

8. How does a revelation of grace—that you're never coming to God in your righteousness but rather in Jesus' righteousness—change your approach to God?

_____

_____

_____

_____

_____

9. What do Romans 8:29, Philippians 2:13, and Philippians 1:6 tell us about how God will shape and mold us?

_____

_____

_____

_____

_____

10. Connection to God is the only way to transformation. How does Romans 8:5–8 make it clear that you cannot _will_ yourself into being a fruitful Christian who lives righteously?

_____

_____

_____

_____

11. Only renewing your mind to the truth about grace can make you righteousness-conscious. But what happens when we feel we *ought* to have a daily quiet time with God in order to make that happen?

_____

_____

_____

_____

12. How does having the mindset of a daughter or son change our view of fellowship with our Father? Why is it that only the truth about grace fosters an intimate, ongoing, life-connection to God?

_____

_____

_____

_____

_____

13. Romans 12:2 makes it clear that the "renewing of your mind" produces the transformation that keeps you from being "conformed to this world." But to what are you renewing your mind?

_____

_____

_____

_____

14. In Romans 6:1–3, how does Paul answer the question of the "license to sin" argument?

_____

_____

_____

_____

_____

15. How is Jesus' statement in John 15:5 the key to changing your "wanter"? What will keep you from that?

_____

_____

_____

_____

_____

_____

16. What does it mean that the scribes and the Pharisees were reading the Bible at the wrong tree? What was the tragic result?

_____

_____

_____

_____

_____

_____

17. How is it even possible that we can read our Bible in the light of the "Tree of Life"? What happens when we do?

_____

_____

_____

_____

_____

18. List some of the ways God's grace is woven into practically every page of the Bible.

_____

_____

_____

_____

_____

19. Just as there were *two* trees in the Garden of Eden, and just as the father in Jesus' parable had *two* sons, what are the *two* options for living the Christian life?

_____

_____

_____

_____

20. Based upon what you have learned in this book, write a bold statement on making "Grace, Period" the foundational truth out of which you live your Christian life.

ABOUT THE AUTHOR

ROBERT MORRIS is the senior pastor of Gateway Church, a multicampus church based in the Dallas–Fort Worth Metroplex. Since it began in 2000, the church has grown to more than 100,000 active attendees. His television program airs in over 190 countries, and his radio program, *Worship & the Word with Pastor Robert*, airs in more than 6,800 cities. He serves as chancellor of The King's University and is the bestselling author of numerous books, including *The Blessed Life*, *Frequency*, *Beyond Blessed*, and *Take the Day Off*. Robert and his wife, Debbie, have been married forty-three years and are blessed with one married daughter, two married sons, and nine grandchildren.